XXXXXXXXX

Especially for

_____

From

_____

Date

_____

XXXXXXXXX

Published by Barbour Publishing, Inc., P.O. Box 719, Uhrichsville, Ohio 44683, www.barbourbooks.com

Our mission is to publish and distribute inspirational products offering exceptional value and biblical encouragement to the masses.

Member of the
Evangelical Christian
Publishers Association

Inspiring Thoughts
for
Quilters

Patricia Mitchell

BARBOUR
PUBLISHING

Contents

Introduction:
What We Love about Quilting

Quilts! They're gifts of function and beauty, of hands and heart—and each one has a story to tell.

Quilts passed down to us tell of quilters who have gone before us. Their handiwork reflects their practical household needs and their desire to bring beauty and color into even the most humble of homes. In the quilts of history, we glimpse the silent loneliness of a woman stitching by lamplight far into the night, and we hear the chattering voices of friends gathered around a frame, each woman with a needle in hand. It's their skills, creativity, innovation, and imagination that set the foundation of the quilts we make and admire today.

Like all generations of quilters, we bring new techniques, new materials, new ideas, and new perspectives to the ancient art. The quilts we make echo our passions and joys, and they reveal our needs, ideals, and values. With each stitch we take, with each innovation we make, we're continuing the legacy of quilts and quiltmakers the world over.

SECTION 1

×××××××××××××××××

Threads
of Tradition

One generation will commend your works to another; they will tell of your mighty acts.

PSALM 145:4 NIV

An Ancient Art

Many women of Bible times were outstanding needlework artists.

In all probability, the Israelites learned the art of fancy stitchery when they were in Egypt, a land long renown for fine linens and skilled needlework artists. The Jewish women, then, would have passed down their expertise to future generations. The richly embroidered designs that adorned tabernacle linens, as well as the garments of priests and wealthy men and women, attest to the women's proficiency and creativity.

Seams Wonderful:
Block Quilts

The Patchwork Girl, who accompanied Dorothy along the yellow-brick road in *The Wonderful Wizard of Oz* by L. Frank Baum, is a truly American creation. In the late nineteenth century when Baum wrote the children's classic, patchwork soared in popularity as small-scale prints became affordable and widely available, thanks to advances in cloth-making techniques. Quilters thrilled over the endless patterns possible in a stack of calico squares!

One-, four-, or nine-patch blocks were used to create elegantly simple patterns with alternating light and dark patches, and intriguingly complex patterns of repeating blocks to create visual symmetry and the illusion of dimension. Many extant quilts reveal careful planning on the part of the quilter. Sometimes her patterns are quite obvious, and other times they're a delightful discovery for the attentive viewer.

Fabric left over? Frugal quilters devised ingenious ways to use scraps. The popular charm quilt was one—the style called for 999 different prints, none repeated.

Though the flash and dazzle, the artistry and intricacy of prize-winning designs amaze, it's okay for any quilter or quilter wannabe to say, "That's not me—yet." With a stack of squares, anyone can create a pretty and pleasing block quilt to use, enjoy, and pass down to the next generation—a beautiful quilt to tickle the seams of all patchwork gals!

Seams Precise

Tape a sliver of straight-cut paper or a piece of yarn to your sewing machine face plate to help achieve an accurate ¼-inch seam allowance.

LESLIE MOLNAR-GRABOWSKI

Quality Quilting

Don't scrimp on sewing equipment, including lighting. Buy the best you can afford. Good equipment makes the process a pleasure, not a frustration.

ROSEMARY VAN HAAREN

Fatal Attraction

If you have a computerized machine, avoid using magnetized pin boxes or similar accessories on or near your machine. A magnet can interfere with the operation of the machine.

MOLLY L. LISTER

Squared Away

Here's an easy way to make a square within a square block: Select a size for the center block, then cut two more squares the same size. These will be for the corners.

Cut the two squares diagonally twice to make four triangles.

Sew a triangle to two opposite sides of the center block; press seams away from center.

Sew the remaining two triangles to the center block and press.

Trim the block down to size (don't forget to leave a ¼-inch seam allowance on all four sides).

Jo Crabb

Good Purchases

When you're looking for compatible fabrics for a current project, make swatches of fabric you already have and keep the swatches in your purse. It will take the guesswork out of mixing and matching as you shop.

Alison Jones

Inspired by History:
Colonial Revival Quilts

While some quilters are always on the lookout for new techniques and innovative ideas, other quilters turn to the past for their inspiration.

In the early twentieth century, a wave of nostalgia for the perceived balance and order of an era gone by swept America. Quilters, no less than architects and interior decorators, took their creative cue from their colonial forebears, and the Colonial Revival style was born.

Women's magazines of the 1920s featured patterns for quilts based on the designs of quilts that had been handed down in American families since the seventeenth century. Along with patterns, the magazines offered sentimental stories of the women who made the original quilts, and invited readers to create their own quilts as heirlooms for their daughters and granddaughters to cherish.

As is true with other styles revived by a later generation, Colonial Revival quilters brought their

own slant and interpretation to the traditional colonial motifs. The availability of modern fabric colors gave old-fashioned designs a fresh look, and the readiness of quilters to revise and adapt to fit their own sense of beauty and style brought new life to a historic pattern.

Quilts from colonial times inspire quilters to this day as we look to our foremothers and forefathers for wisdom, guidance, and direction.

Of Thimbles, Thread, and Faith

"My grandma is teaching me how to quilt," the young woman said. The light in her eyes and the excitement in her voice showed she was a ready learner! She might already have realized that her grandmother was passing on a lifetime gift—a love of quilting.

In the same way, the Holy Spirit uses the love we have for God as a tool to draw the younger generation to faith. It's our example young people see, it's our words they hear, it's the pattern of our lives that piques their interest. They come to realize we have something special—peace, patience, joy, generosity, hope—and they want to know more. They start asking questions. They want to learn for themselves what it is we know that gives us the confidence we possess in Him.

"Will you show me how to do that?" are words quilting grandmas, moms, aunts, and friends delight to hear, and we're only too happy to pull up another chair, get out another needle, and show the eager learner how it's done. We smile to know we're passing on not simply the warmth and comfort of a quilt but also the joy of creating it. And we are blessed even more when we share something far more important than the quilt—the warmth, comfort, and joy of faith in Jesus Christ.

Come, O children, listen to me;
I will teach you the fear of the LORD.

Psalm 34:11 ESV

In the Beginning

In the Old Testament, we meet Rahab of Jericho, who protected two Israelite spies by leading them up to her flat roof and hiding them under piles of flax (Joshua 2:6).

After harvest, flax stalks were soaked in water to soften them, then taken up to the roof to dry. The stalks broke into fibers, which were separated, spun, and woven into linen. Linen cloth could be left its natural off-white color or dyed. Popular colors were achieved using the rind of pomegranates, the bark of trees, or various herbs and roots.

An American Icon:
The Log Cabin Quilt

How many patterns can you stitch with a stack of strips? It's the Log Cabin challenge!

Created by joining narrow strips of increasing lengths around a central square, simple Log Cabin patterns allow novice quilters to learn the art of accurate cutting and straight-seam sewing as they create precise geometric blocks. More complex Log Cabin patterns challenge experienced quilters, as these designs can require painstaking planning and detailed workmanship. So skillful and imaginative were Log Cabin quilters of the late nineteenth century, and so popular the design style, that Log Cabin quilts gained a category to themselves at state fairs and community needlework competitions.

Log Cabin designs, and their Pineapple and Courthouse Steps variations, rely on a combination of light and dark strips to create visual interest and contrast. While stunning effects can be achieved using a limited number of fabrics throughout the quilt, many Log Cabins incorporate a variety of fabrics with very pleasing results.

Like our pioneer forebears who built log cabins log by log, Log Cabin quilters achieve their fabulous results strip by strip. While the era of log cabins is behind us, Log Cabin quilts remain a quilter's favorite to this day. So, start stripping!

Pretty in Reverse

Give your quilt backs a splash of color and creativity by piecing together lengths of fabric left over from the quilt top, along with other coordinating fabrics. (Very often, if you've purchased a fat-quarter or half-yard bundle, you're left with an unused panel or two. Add them to the quilt back!)

ALISON JONES

Scrappy Smiles

After completing a sewing project, make two-inch, half-square triangles from the fabric scraps. Set aside. When you've gathered enough from other projects, put all the squares together to create a scrappy quilt! This is especially great when making a quilt to donate or as a gift, since much of the piecing is already done.

LESLIE MOLNAR-GRABOWSKI

Flat Fit

At your favorite pizza shop, ask if you can buy a few new unused pizza boxes. These make perfect storage boxes as you complete the blocks of a block-of-the-month quilt or other long-term project. Label each one if you have several works in progress (and who doesn't?).

MOLLY L. LISTER

Going Batty

Leftover batting makes packing material for mailing fragile items, as well as for storing breakables.

ALISON JONES

Strategic Planning

If your quilt will be displayed folded at the foot of a bed, across the back of a sofa, or on a quilt rack, place your favorite squares where they will be seen, rather than hidden in the folds.

ANNE THOMSSEN

Less Is More:
Quilts in Miniature

So many quilts and so little time! For the satisfaction of completing a quilt more quickly, many quilters today are turning to quilts in miniature.

Traditionally, a miniature quilt is a 1:12 ratio reproduction of a classic design—that is, a twelve-inch block of the original quilt is reduced to a one-inch block for the miniature. These charming quilts grace the beds of many well-appointed dollhouses, but not all quilts that qualify as miniature are doll-bed size.

A miniature quilt can be any smaller version of a full-size quilt. When used as a wall hanging, a miniature may reproduce the original on a 2:12 or even a 4:12 ratio, where a twelve-inch block of the original becomes a two- or four-inch block of its diminutive daughter. Quilters who want to learn the classic patterns of a historical piece without investing the time and expense

of making a full quilt may find a miniature version an attractive option.

While quilt shows set rules for quilts qualifying for the miniature category, you are free to design, adapt, and measure as you please for a captivating miniature quilt. Though it won't drape over a queen-size bed, a miniature quilt is something its more expansive mama may not be for quite some time: *finished*!

Gift of the Past

It's tempting to imagine past decades, past eras, as times simpler than our own. We think people living then did not have to deal with all the things we have to deal with, from hectic schedules to climate change. We may even suppose discipleship was easier. After all, did the first Christians live in cultures as immoral as our own?

The answer is yes, they did. The dominant culture of the time embraced a plethora of false gods and heathen idols. The decadence of Roman emperors was widely known, corruption among local officials was rampant, cities were centers of disease, and the roads between them were the domain of thugs and bandits. During the time of the early church, Christians faced these fears, as well as persecution, and sometimes death, for their faith.

When we realize what our spiritual mothers and fathers, sisters and brothers were up against, we're not apt to romanticize them but to be inspired by them. Their faithfulness to their risen Lord permeated their decisions and strengthened their resolve to follow in His way. Their day-to-day endurance set the pattern for believers of all times, and we are the inheritors of their example.

Today, in our culture and in our time, our thoughts, words, and actions reflect what God has set down of old for the good of His people of all times.

So then, just as you received
Christ Jesus as Lord,
continue to live in him,
rooted and built up in him,
strengthened in the faith
as you were taught, and
overflowing with thankfulness.

COLOSSIANS 2:6–7 NIV

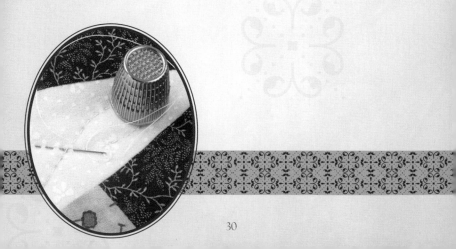

SECTION 2

xxxxxxxxxxxxxxxxxx

Designed to Inspire

Come and hear, all you who fear
God, and I will declare what He has
done for my soul.

PSALM 66:16 NKJV

Whole Cloth

As Jesus hung on the cross, soldiers divided His garments among themselves—evidence of how prized clothing was in those days. Jesus' tunic, however, "was without seam, woven from the top in one piece" (John 19:23 NKJV), and even these hardened men were loath to tear it apart. Instead, they threw dice to determine who won it.

The large loom needed to weave a one-piece tunic was a recent innovation, and seamless garments were not common possessions of ordinary people. Undoubtedly, Jesus' tunic was presented to Him as a gift by one of his devoted (and moneyed) followers.

Fabric of Faith:
Scripture Quilts

Home and church dominated the lives of most nineteenth-century American women. If no other book could be found in the home, there would be a Bible, and the first stories children heard were read from its pages. At church, even women who couldn't read heard sermons and, in many cases, learned major stories and significant concepts through religious icons and symbols they saw. It isn't surprising, then, that what women heard, learned, and saw at church inspired their quilting patterns at home!

Flowers from the Bible were a common theme for appliquéd quilts, and none was more popular than the Rose of Sharon pattern, which was often used on a quilt made as a wedding gift. Other appliquéd and embroidered quilts might illustrate a series of Bible stories with representational figures, or center on one narrative. Pieced quilts depicted biblical symbols, and block names, such as Crown of Thorns, Devil's Claws, Cross and Crown, and Carpenter's Wheel, reveal their sacred origins.

Popular today are quilt designs that incorporate Bible verses, either hand or machine embroidered or inscribed in fabric-friendly permanent ink. These expressions of faith are frequently made for the comfort, encouragement, and inspiration of friends facing a major illness or going through treatment.

Whatever the style or method used, scripture quilts express faith, share the Word, and witness to the enduring power of God's creative Spirit at work in our lives.

Charmingly Organized

Wooden picnic baskets with lids are excellent containers for fabrics, scraps, and tools. Choose different sizes to give your sewing room a decorative look.

LESLIE MOLNAR-GRABOWSKI

Sharp Point 1

Be sure to change the sewing machine needle frequently. A new, sharp needle makes the stitching so much easier. You may be able to use the same needle on several small projects, but you may need to use several needles on a large project.

ROSEMARY VAN HAAREN

Sharp Point 2

Pins kept in wool pincushions don't rust and are kept sharp in the wool's lanolin.

SHARYN RIGG

Just for You

Introduce a preteen to quilting by preparing a personalized kit for a quilted throw or wall hanging. Into a zippered bag or tote, pack:

> 81 4½-inch squares in favorite colors or prints
> 2 36-inch strips for top and bottom borders, 4½ inches wide
> 2 44-inch strips for side borders, 4½ inches wide
> 5 yards quilt binding
> 50-inch square batting
> 50-inch square backing
> one-ply yarn for ties
> fabric label
> instructions for piecing patches and border, adding binding, batting, and finishing (plus your own tips!).

Finished quilt: 44-inch square

ALISON JONES

Kaleidoscope of Color:
Mariner's Compass Quilts

Though its name dates back to only the twentieth century, the Mariner's Compass is one of the earliest known quilt designs.

Most likely inspired by the compass rose design that graced nautical maps of the known world (and before the compass, the wind rose design), skilled needlewomen replicated the design in their quilts. Early names for the pattern include Starburst, Explosion, and Rising Sun, all apt appellations for 16 to 32 geometric rays bursting from a center circle or point. A pieced Mariner's Compass design, once complete, is set within a larger circle, typically bordered by additional patchwork patterns.

Each ray of a traditional Mariner's Compass is composed of at least two pieces, one dark and one light, often intersecting smaller rays of two (or more) different light/dark combinations. With careful planning, the finished pattern gives the illusion of a multi-dimensional surface, drawing the eye from the center out and around the design.

A Mariner's Compass quilt is not for the faint-of-heart. Its precise points, complex pattern, and exacting piecing requirements take skill, but with practice, you can master the pattern. As you beam with well-deserved pride in front of your completed Compass, know you've reached a quilting milestone—and you're ready for anything now!

Way to Go

You're eager to start a new quilting project, so you get out your stash and start looking through it. With all your fabric laid out in front of you, though, your enthusiasm fades. Should you go for a traditional or modern look? Bright or muted color scheme? Easy or intricate pattern? So many choices!

Our lives, too, offer us an astounding array of choices. Each day, we pick and choose from a great number of options open to us. Sometimes, however, the many choices available to us can lead us to choose the wrong direction.

God has given us the Bible as a compass to guide us through and among our choices. His commandments point us to the right path, and His gospel leads us toward His forgiveness, mercy, and love. The wisdom we receive from His Spirit at work in us as we read and study His Word guides us along the way He would have us go in every season of life.

Ask the Holy Spirit to give your life direction. Allow Him to guide you toward God-pleasing choices. And if the way gets complicated or the choices overwhelming, put your trust in Him. Rest at ease in knowing that God has chosen you.

In all your ways acknowledge Him,
and He shall direct your paths.

PROVERBS 3:6 NKJV

Embellished to Envy

Israel (Jacob) presented his favorite son, Joseph, with a splendid coat. Just what made the coat so splendid, however, is an open question.

The Hebrew word used to describe the coat could be translated in various ways: many colors, richly ornamented, long-sleeved, and, according to the title of a popular musical, technicolor! Whatever the needlework marvel involved, the coat was the catalyst God used to start Joseph on his remarkable life's journey of hardship, challenge, temptation, and, in the end, extraordinary honor, influence, and power.

A Little of This, a Little of That: Sampler Quilts

If you like variety, a Sampler quilt is for you. Indeed, a well-brought-up young lady of the nineteenth century would make a Sampler quilt to show off her finesse with a needle. The girl's work was artfully displayed in the parlor to impress her suitors and enhance her desirability as a wife.

Today, many quilters undertake a Sampler quilt to learn different quilting techniques, as each block incorporates a different style. Some quilters include appliquéd along with pieced blocks in their Sampler quilts, offering them an opportunity to practice yet another quilting skill. From experience with a Sampler quilt, a quilter may discover the colorways, techniques, or methods that inspire a lifelong passion.

Some Sampler quilts are a group effort. Drawing from the same collection of fabrics, each quilter creates a block according to her own vision. Each block highlights the creativity and skills of the individual quilter, yet all the blocks work together delightfully once they're

arranged and joined with complementary sashing and borders. In many cases, the individual quilters sign their blocks, a tribute to their common cause.

Especially for beginners, Sampler quilts are fun to sew and provide a wealth of hands-on experience—and whether you're in the market for marriage or not, a decorative Sampler is guaranteed to win admiring glances from all who come to call.

Shining Success

When sewing with metallic threads on your sewing machine, don't forget to use a needle made for these threads. A regular needle will cause metallic threads to break easily.

ALISON JONES

Right Size, Right Price

Can't find the size ruler you need? Found the ruler, but the price made you gasp? You can get the exact sizes you need for far less money by going to your favorite hardware store. Buy a sheet of Plexiglas and ask them to cut the sizes you need. When you get home, label each ruler for easy use.

Note: To get the extra service, it helps to go on a day the store is not busy. And be sure to thank the clerk who cut these for you, as you may want to do this again for your next project!

JO CRABB

Reuse, Recycle

Line the bottom of an empty CD jewel case with a block of felt or thin batting:

> It's a great carrier for pins and needles when you're stitching on the go.
>
> It's a safe place to keep small appliqué pieces.
>
> It's the right-sized design wall for the blocks of an in-progress miniature quilt.

ALISON JONES

Oops!

If you accidentally snip a small hole in your quilt top, cover it creatively with a tiny appliqué motif, such as a butterfly, flower, bumblebee, or abstract shape.

ANNE THOMSSEN

Get a Grip

To mark the diagonal of a square, lay a square rubber jar gripper from point to point. It grips the fabric and lets you mark without stretching the bias.

DENICE LACKEY

Center Attraction:
Medallion Quilts

When your eyes fly straight to the center design of a quilt, chances are you're looking at a Medallion quilt.

Medallion quilts are planned around a dominant center design. The center, or focal point, may consist of a bold embroidered or appliquéd motif, an interesting printed panel, or an intricate patchwork design, such as a star or diamond. The rest of the quilt's pattern

emanates from the focal point, echoing its theme, color, style, and mood.

American colonists brought medallion-style quilts from England and the Netherlands, where quilts were traditionally planned around a central design, and Medallion quilts remain popular with quilters today. While early Medallion quilts can be visually busy and technically complicated, contemporary Medallion quilts often combine the medallion tradition with simple, contemporary designs and fabrics for stunning results.

If there's a printed fabric in your stash that you love but don't know how to use in a quilt, a medallion design could be your answer. Or if a past project has left you with an orphaned block, it's a Medallion quilt waiting to happen. Just frame the block with complementary fabrics and designs, and voilà—a Medallion quilt! After all, once you have a great centerpiece, all the rest is just a matter of adding on.

Front and Center

From a simple appliquéd heart to a delicately drawn garden print, you can't miss the focus of a Medallion quilt. It's front and center, for all to see.

Our lives, too, need to have that kind of clear and discernable focus. Without focus, our plans and actions are apt to work against each other, creating frustration and confusion. Without focus, we're prone to add to our lives whatever attracts us at the moment, whether or not it supports our values and goals. When we fail to define our focus, our purpose in life becomes as tangled as the thread of a runaway spool.

From Mount Sinai, God gave us our focus: "You shall have no other gods before Me" (Exodus 20:3 NKJV). God tolerates no competing designs and no rival patterns in our lives. He will not remain as a supporting block in service to some other dominant interest.

Think of your life as a Medallion quilt. God is the centerpiece, without question. All your blessings and talents highlight His goodness in your life. All your thoughts, words, and actions support His purpose for your life. As for those who see you? They can't miss Him, because He's right there, front and center!

Thou shalt love the Lord
thy God with all thy heart,
and with all thy soul,
and with all thy strength,
and with all thy mind;
and thy neighbour as thyself.

LUKE 10:27 KJV

SECTION 3

×××××××××××××××××

Smiles in Stitches

A happy heart makes
the face cheerful.

PROVERBS 15:13 NIV

Epyptian Linen

In Old Testament times, linen from Egypt rated right up there with rare gems and expensive perfumes.

While flax, from which linen is made, grew in abundance along the coasts of Canaan and in the hills of Galilee, the finest linen was imported from Egypt. This fabric, softened through a process the Egyptians guarded jealously, was beyond the means of ordinary folk. Beautifully dyed and richly decorated, Egyptian linen clothed kings and princes and adorned the palaces of the wealthy.

Whimsical Work:
Yo-Yo Quilts

Quilters of the early twentieth century go *down* in history for coming *up* with the Yo-yo quilt.

A yo-yo is made with a small circle of fabric, often traced from a spool end, jar lid, or drinking glass rim. A running stitch is sewn around the circle's edge, then the threads are drawn to close the circle, which is then flattened to form the yo-yo.

At the height of yo-yo mania in the 1930s, yo-yos by the dozens, hundreds, or even thousands were linked together to create a pattern, scene, or abstract design. Some yo-yo aficionados would add a button or French knot in the middle of each yo-yo for further visual impact. Other quilters stuffed a pinch of batting inside each yo-yo for added depth and dimension. Since the thread-linked yo-yos usually had no backing, the finished piece was delicate and not warm. A Yo-yo quilt was generally used during summer months, spread over a sheet as a decorative coverlet for the bed.

Though bed-size Yo-yo quilts have waned in popularity, yo-yos themselves continue to bob around the quilting scene. Today yo-yos may be made into decorative throws, pillows, or table runners; or they may be grouped together and added as playful appliqué "flowers" to vests, jackets, tote bags, and sweatshirts. Wherever they're used, they're sure to bring a smile!

Quick Visual

Store fabric in clear containers so you can see at a glance what you have. To fold lengths of fabric to a uniform size, use a four-inch or six-inch ruler. Fold each piece around the ruler, then pull the ruler out and stack.

ANNE THOMSSEN

Love the Label!

Don't let your creativity stop when you label your quilt! Create a frame for your information using scraps from your project, or appliqué a frame using a motif from the quilt top.

ALISON JONES

Ruler Rule

Be consistent with the way you measure, taking into consideration the thickness of your ruler's lines. Even a slight variation can make a significant difference in the finished size of your quilt.

MOLLY L. LISTER

Good Threads

Be sure to thread your needle on the end of the thread as it comes off the spool. Knot the end where you cut it off the spool. That way, your thread is less likely to twist and knot as you sew.

SHARYN RIGG

Quilts in Color

Use children's coloring books as a resource for fun appliqué designs!

LESLIE MOLNAR-GRABOWSKI

A Fabulous Confection:
Crazy Quilts

In the late 1800s, Crazy quilts were the rage in America. Was this an aesthetic reaction to the post-Civil War popularity of geometric patterns, or a determination among frugal quilters to use up scraps of lace, brocade, corduroy, velvet, and taffeta? Either way, the result is always novel and often stunning.

Crazy quilts, with their lopsided shapes and seeming hodgepodge of fabrics, textures, and trimmings, are among the most individual and expressive of quilt styles. A Crazy quilt typically includes personal memorabilia, such as award ribbons, patches from organizations, scraps from favorite dresses, and fabric pieces signed by family members and friends.

If you want to make a traditional Crazy quilt, you're not finished after you've joined all your curious and sundry pieces together—oh no! Each connecting seam has to be topped with fancy embroidery stitches, using an assortment of threads, yarns, and flosses. Then you'll want to further embellish your work with embroidered stars, flowers, birds, dogs, cats, or exotic animals, as well as religious, patriotic, or special-interest motifs. To that add sequins, beads, buttons, decals, shells, pictures, tassels—and a spider web to ensure good luck!

For fun, creativity, and a chance to revisit favorite memories, you couldn't do better than a Crazy quilt. (And by the way, *Crazy* refers to the crisscross, asymmetrical, "crazed" lines of the quilt, not to the mental state of the quilter!)

Happy Today

Before the advent of inexpensive and widely available fabrics in the mid-1800s, most quiltmakers used what they had. They counted themselves happy to have scraps left over from dressmaking, or usable fabric from the family's old clothes. Their quilts were not only necessary for their warmth and comfort but were often artistically planned and beautifully finished.

God has seen fit to bless us with many happy things, readily and easily available to us. Since our bedding is store-bought, we make quilts because we love to make quilts. Rather than having to go through our closets to ferret out used pieces of cloth, we stroll through the aisles of a well-stocked fabric store and buy all we want (well, *almost* all we want!).

We turn the happiness God wants for us wrong-side-out, however, when we forget to give Him thanks for what we have. When we cannot look around us and smile at His goodness to us, we've lost the essence of joy.

Sometimes we do our most beautiful and creative work when we follow the path of quilters who used what they had because of necessity, but used it all with skill, creativity, and grace. Sometimes we don't need to gather more but to see with joyful gratitude what we already have.

"I will send down
the showers in their season;
they shall be showers of blessing."

Ezekiel 34:26 ESV

Joy Bringer

After the resurrection of Jesus and during the years of the apostles, a community of Christians grew up in the seaport city of Joppa.

One member of this community, Dorcas (also called Tabitha), was a seamstress by profession and a bringer of joy to others. "She was full of good works and acts of charity" (Acts 9:36 ESV), and it is likely she used her sewing skills to make garments that she could donate to the poor.

Leaping Flames:
Bargello Quilts

The Bargello design is an interior decorating staple. The colorful flame-stitch pattern is created with a series of stepped vertical stitches, resembling an inverted V—or flame—motif. While machine-made now, originally Bargello was hand-embroidered with wool thread on canvas. Either way it's produced, the Bargello technique creates a strong, durable fabric, superb for chair cushions, furniture upholstery, drapery, and fine carpets.

Bargello, commonly thought to have originated in Florence in the seventeenth century, retains a following among embroiders to this day. The challenging stitch requires accuracy in thread-counting to achieve a uniform flame pattern and takes concentration and practice to achieve the desired results.

Bargello quilting, however, can be a beginner's dream come true. Though a Bargello quilt design may appear as complicated as its embroidered counterpart, it isn't!

A simple Bargello quilt is constructed by sewing strips of fabrics together, then cutting the piece crosswise into multi-colored blocks of varying lengths. The blocks are then arranged to form the distinctive stepped Bargello motif and then sewn together to create a quilt.

With strips of fabrics, a ruler, cutter, and sewing machine, even a novice quilter can create a colorful, captivating, and complicated-looking Bargello quilt!

Picture This!

Make your own design wall by covering a piece of foam board, plywood, or cork board with low-pile batting. When arranging fabric pieces on the design wall, it often helps to keep them up for several days, allowing you to see how the colors work together in both natural and artificial light.

ALISON JONES

Free Fabric

Get your quilting friends together for a scrap swap! What's been lying at the bottom of someone else's scrap basket might be just the thing that inspires your next quilting project.

ANNE THOMSSEN

Share the Passion

Take a photo of your latest quilt and print the picture on a postcard or card stock. On the back, note your name, the name of the quilt, and any other information. Let your friends see your handiwork!

ANNE THOMSSEN

Roll-Ups

When you make fabric bias strips for appliqué stems and borders, roll the strip around an empty bathroom tissue core. This way, your strip will stay flat and ready for use.

MOLLY L. LISTER

Home Show

If you like to rotate small quilts or quilt wall hangings around your home, use clear thumb tacks. When you're ready to remove the quilt from the wall, simply rub the bowl of a spoon over the puncture, and it disappears.

LESLIE MOLNAR-GRABOWSKI

Optical Illusions:
Mosaic Patchwork

Mosaic tile designs date back to ancient times. Perhaps inspired by designs that graced temples, palaces, and public squares, quiltmakers joined tiny fabric "tiles" together to create highly stylized scenes and enchanting geometric patterns.

Today mosaic patchwork is done using paper, board, or acrylic templates. The quiltmaker cuts templates to exact size, wraps a piece of fabric around each one, firmly bastes fabric in place, then whipstitches each fabric tile to its neighbor. After the seams are secure, the templates are removed. The result? A series of perfectly angled, flat, crisp textile tiles!

Engaging Mosaic quilts might consist of hundreds of tiny hexagons or diamonds joined together. Through the use of various colors and tile patterns, the quilter can create eye-catching patterns of visual balance and design symmetry, or a picture depicting an object or scene.

Especially clever planning on the part of the

quiltmaker is evident in the complex designs of some Mosaic quilts. These quilts may feature a main pattern and a secondary pattern (sometimes subtle) repeated throughout the quilt, or a realistically rendered picture with shading and perspective. In many cases, the individual tiles are so small that no overall quilting is added to the completed piece.

A Mosaic quilt is a happy way to use up all those little scraps you've saved all these years!

Patterns of Life

The many and varied events of your life may seem no more connected than an array of quilt blocks strewn across your sewing table. Some blocks you like—the colors and patterns please you, and you'll happily connect them together. Those are the good times when things were going smoothly, the happy times shared with those you love.

Other blocks, however, appeal to you less. You don't like them because you think they're ugly, and you don't want them part of the quilt you plan to title "My Life." Those are the times that could have been better—the times when things did not work out the way you wanted them to; when illness put a hold on your plans; when one heartache followed another. Yet these blocks, too, have a God-given place in the pattern of your days.

Just as quilters use the contrast of bright and dark, solid and print, plain and decorative to create quilts of depth and vibrancy, God uses all the patterns in your life for good. A troubling event set next to the lesson you learned deepens experience and wisdom.

A joyful occasion set next to a time of sorrow develops compassion and understanding. The time you needed forgiveness, set next to the forgiveness you extended to others.

These are the building blocks God uses to make your life what it is—a precious gift from the Master quilter to you.

To every thing there is a season,
and a time to every purpose
under the heaven.

ECCLESIASTES 3:1 KJV

SECTION 4

xxxxxxxxxxxxxxxxxx

Soul of Expression

Now there are varieties of gifts,
but the same Spirit; and there are
varieties of service, but the same Lord.

1 CORINTHIANS 12:4–5 ESV

From Flax to Finish

The Woman of Proverbs 31 knew her way around fabric.
She gathered and dried the flax, and she wove her cloth.
She sewed clothes for herself and her family, along with
the family's bedding. In addition, she made garments
to sell!

While some quilters today strive to do it all, from
designing and dying the fabric to quilting the very last
stitch, in past generations the tasks were commonly
divided. A wealthy woman would buy the fabric
and stitch the quilt top, doing the piecing and fancy
needlework. She would then pay to have a woman quilt
it for her.

The Aloha Spirit:
Hawaiian Quilts

The distinctive look of a Hawaiian quilt grew from a happy fusion of Western methods and materials with native creativity and culture.

When New England missionaries came to the Hawaiian islands in the early 1800s, the women brought with them their fabrics, thread, and quilting traditions. The native women, adept at creating functional and decorative bed coverings with bark cloth and natural dyes, eagerly embraced the new techniques and textiles brought to them from the mainland. The art of appliqué won overwhelming acceptance among islanders, and soon Hawaiian quiltmakers had created their own original quilt patterns and distinctive style. Hawaiian quilts differ from the mainland tradition in three ways:

First, Hawaiian quilts typically consist of only two colors, one for the background (usually white) and one for the appliqué design.

Second, the appliqué design is cut from one piece of fabric folded in fourths or eighths, similar to the way a snowflake is cut out from a sheet of folded paper. There are no small inlaid pieces.

Third, representations of people or animals are not seen on Hawaiian quilts. Hawaiian motifs consist of flowers, trees, or household items.

The intricate appliqué designs of a Hawaiian quilt could take a quilter a long time to stitch—but who cares? The exquisite quilt is more likely to be used for decoration than to keep warm in the winter. After all, this is Hawaii!

Re-Creation Experience

Rather than let a less-than-successful attempt lie at the bottom of your sewing basket, find a way to re-create it:

> Bind an unfinished quilt to make a throw, coverlet, or table topper.
>
> Make a fabric frame for an individual block and apply to a fabric tote, a sweatshirt, an apron, or a throw pillow.
>
> Identify a favorite section of an unfinished project and make a fabric frame for it; display as a wall hanging.
>
> Bind artful strips or block combinations to make a bell pull, table runner, or place mat.
>
> Use small blocks to decorate towels for the kitchen or guest bathroom (these make great hostess gifts, too!).
>
> Stitch appliqué motifs to card stock to use as note cards.

ANNE THOMSSEN

Sit Still, Please!

To keep a square ruler from shifting when you cut around it, apply a small piece of double-sided tape to all four corners before you place it on your fabric. Once you've cut your square, remove the tape immediately to prevent it from drying on the ruler.

ALISON JONES

Thread Right

Needles have a right and wrong side when threading. The thread is accepted more easily through one side than the other. If you're having trouble threading, flip the needle over and try the other side. Also, try wetting the needle instead of the thread when threading a needle.

SHARYN RIGG

Rule of the Rotary

For a clean, accurate cut, rotary blades need to be sharp. When your cutter misses spots on the first cut through the fabric, it's time to change blades.

MOLLY L. LISTER

Patterns of Freedom:
Quilts of Women in Slavery

Before the Civil War, most women quilted, including African-American women in slavery. Often trained as seamstresses, many slave women worked on quilts that would grace their mistress's home, but they created quilts for their own homes as well.

Fabrics a slave woman would have used in her own quilts would have been scraps left over from dressmaking, or those given to her by her mistress, who, in all likelihood, also quilted. The slave woman, however, would have stitched her quilt at night and on her own time, after her field or household duties were done.

Unfortunately, the work of slaves was rarely documented, so historians are unsure about the provenance of unsigned quilts dating from before the Civil War. In addition, few quilts made by slave women for their own families still exist, because these quilts would have been used as day-to-day blankets and bedding. Letters, diaries, and family stories, however, suggest that many existing treasures were made or finished by the hands of enslaved women.

Though her personal circumstances were beyond her control, an enslaved woman gathered what was given to her and with a determined and enduring spirit, created quilts of warmth, security, joy, and hope in a harsh and uncertain world.

Designed by God's Design

You walk into your favorite quilting shop, and you're instantly in love with everything you see—from prairie prints to bright batiks, from funky moderns to romantic florals, from whimsical fairies to classic plaids. Complete bliss for a quilter!

It's not hard to imagine that this is how God feels as He moves among His people. God, who wove each one of us in our mother's womb, designed us to live as distinct and unique persons in appearance, talents, skills, and personality. He delights in our differences and would no more want a world filled with identical people than you would want your quilt shop stocked floor to ceiling with one, and only one, design.

As a quilter, you understand something else, too. You know that it takes more than one design to make a quilt. In fact, some of the most creative, imaginative, and expressive quilts are composed of dozens upon dozens of different fabric designs all working together as one whole quilt. Without one print, no matter how small the piece, or without one color, no matter how tiny the part it plays, the quilt falls short of its creator's vision.

God delights in you precisely because you are different from everyone else. And He knows what quilters know: A unique pattern (you!) shows up best when it's joined with other unique patterns (your family, friends, neighbors, and coworkers). When unique designs work together, great things happen!

O Lord, You are our Father;
we are the clay,
and You our potter;
and all we are the work
of Your hand.

Isaiah 64:8 NKJV

Colorful Business

Lydia was a seller of purple cloth in the city of Philippi. Originally from Thyatira, a town noted for dyeing and garment-making, Lydia would have learned the secret processes involved in achieving a particular shade of purple. Thyatiran purple was made from the madder root and is known today as Turkish red.

A successful businesswoman, Lydia had her own home and servants, along with a heart for hospitality. When Paul was in Philippi, she urged him, saying, "If you have judged me to be faithful to the Lord, come to my house and stay" (Acts 16:15 ESV).

Threads of Life:
The Journal Quilt

As in the past, many quilts today are presented as gifts on special occasions. The quilts, lovingly stitched by family members or close friends, commemorate marriage, the birth of children, graduation, retirement, and other milestone events. A Journal quilt, however, made by the quilter as a gift to herself, celebrates the quilter's life.

Journal quilts, often through representative figures appliquéd within a scene, are purely personal. They may recall a cherished memory, such as the house where the quilter grew up; or highlight a meaningful place, such as a favorite town or vacation spot; or depict dearly loved people, such as family members and friends.

A quilter's Journal quilt conveys deep emotion, too, as she uses shapes and colors to evoke mood and perspective. Happy, vibrant colors tell a whole different story than somber, subtle colors! Judging from the scene depicted or design created, along with the colors employed, the viewer sees in textiles a distinctive point of view.

Usually Journal quilts are much smaller than bed-sized quilts, and they're most often hung on the walls of the quilter's home. Some Journal quilts are smaller, perhaps the size of a sheet of paper, and kept in a loose-leaf binder as a personal diary not in words, but in color and design.

Why not express yourself? All you need to start a Journal quilt is fabric, scissors, and a willingness to say what you think and feel—in stitches!

Keep Bobbin' Along

Set aside a few minutes to wind several white bobbins so
you have one on hand when one runs out. Keep full bobbins
stacked on a straw or a bamboo skewer, then put inside a
small jar next to your sewing machine.

LESLIE MOLNAR-GRABOWSKI

Quick Change Artist

One way to easily switch quilt blocks to reflect the seasons is
to make a basic wall hanging or throw pillow and add Velcro
or snaps to the four corners of the panel and your seasonal
blocks.

ALISON JONES

Handy Basket

Keep a basket on your sewing table with glass jars for small scissors, a seam ripper, ruler, marking pen, etc. That way, all your tools are within easy reach when you're sewing.

LESLIE MOLNAR-GRABOWSKI

Fabric Happy

With each project or favorite fabric find, keep a record of the fabric design or collection, as well as where you bought it. That way, if you need more, you can go directly to the original source.

ANNE THOMSSEN

Good Work!

Separate your usable scraps into piles of complementary color combinations. When you have enough of any one combo, make a strip- or one-block coverlet or quilt and donate it to charity. Colorful quilts make excellent raffle items!

MOLLY L. LISTER

Quilting Outside the Pattern:
Art Quilts

While all quilting can be regarded as a form of self-expression—even quilts constructed from a kit reveal an individual quilter's personal touch—Art quilts carry the concept to the limits.

Developed in the late 1970s, Art quilters threw out traditional quilting "rules" in favor of self-expression, discovery, and innovation. Cottons gave way to textiles of all kinds, and techniques tried included stitchery, painting, calligraphy, and inventive add-ons. In the 1980s, Art quilts started to receive recognition in the art world as well as in the quilting world, and major exhibitions of Art quilts are still controversial, but not uncommon.

Today Art quilters are multimedia artists, bringing to quilting whatever has captured their interest at the moment—computer technology, new materials, and as-yet-untried experiments in dimension, depth, and scale. While an Art quilt may be the size of a small wall hanging, it can also cover the entire wall, side to side, floor to ceiling!

Like Journal quilts, Art quilts carry a message from the creator to the viewer. Art quilts, however, take what's personal and translate it to what's universal. Many Art quilts comment on world events and life's realities through abstract images, colors, and design treatments, making a statement intended to evoke a response from a wide and varied audience.

If you love quilting but also love painting, dyeing, video, printing, and computers, an Art quilt is something you might want to try. And don't worry about following the rules—because there aren't any!

The Comfort of Quilts

Sure, quilts serve a practical purpose, but we especially appreciate quilts because they do so much more. From generation to generation, quilts have evoked the pleasing feelings of love and caring, of beauty and gentleness. While offering warmth for the body, quilts provide warmth for the soul.

God's Word works in us and for us in a similar way. Certainly His commandments are designed to achieve a practical purpose. Their warnings offer protection from danger to body and soul, and they show us the way God would have us to go. Without His commandments, we would be left out in the cold, with no firm knowledge of God's will for our lives.

We know, however, that God's Word does so much more. His gospel envelops us in God's love through the life, death, and resurrection of His Son, Jesus Christ. God's forgiveness and His promises cover our lives with comfort and hope, and His Spirit adorns our hearts with His gifts of goodness, peace, patience, and love.

Truly the most exquisite "quilt" you will ever see is the one God has given to you in the Bible. Let your Lord enfold you in His Word, His practical and pleasing gift to you each day.

Whether you eat or drink
or whatever you do,
do it all for the glory of God.

1 CORINTHIANS 10:31 NIV

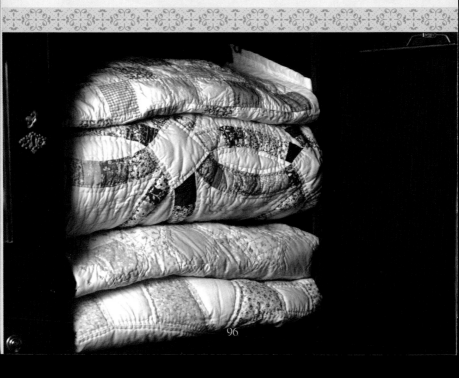